EXTREME

Toxic!

Killer Cures and Other Poisonings

Susie Hodge

A & C Black • London

WARNING!
Never try to make
poisons or cures yourself.

This book is produced using paper that is made
from wood grown in managed, sustainable forests.
It is natural, renewable and recyclable. The logging
and manufacturing processes conform to the
environmental regulations of the country of origin.

Printed in China by C & C Offset Printing Co., Ltd

Produced for A & C Black by
Monkey Puzzle Media Ltd
The Rectory, Eyke, Woodbridge
Suffolk IP12 2QW, UK

Published by A & C Black Publishers Limited
38 Soho Square, London W1D 3HB

First published 2008
Copyright © 2008 A & C Black Publishers Limited

ISBN 978-1-4081-0020-2 (hardback)
ISBN 978-1-4081-0100-1 (paperback)

A CIP catalogue record for this book is available
from the British Library.

Editor: Cath Senker
Design: Mayer Media Ltd
Picture research: Lynda Lines
Series consultant: Jane Turner

Picture acknowledgements
akg-images pp. 4, 7, 24 (Ullstein Bild/Lieberenz);
Alamy pp. 9 bottom (NAS Medical), 15 (Lebrecht
Music and Arts Photo Library), 19 (John McKenna);
Art Archive pp. 10 (British Museum/Eileen Tweedy),
13 (Issogne Castle, Val d'Aosta/Alfredo Dagli Orti),
16, 18 (Bibliotheque des Arts Décoratifs,
Paris/Gianni Dagli Orti), 21 (Private Collection,
Paris/Gianni Dagli Orti), 22 (Musée d'Orsay,
Paris/Gianni Dagli Orti), 25 (Musée du Château de
Versailles/Gianni Dagli Orti); Corbis pp. 1 (Sucheta
Das/Reuters), 5 (Sucheta Das/Reuters), 6 (Alfried
Krecichwost/Zefa), 11 (Bettmann), 20 (Historical
Picture Archive), 23 (Sonja Pancho/Zefa), 28
(Anthony Bannister), 29 top (Kapoor Baldev); Getty
Images pp. 9 top (Burazin), 27 both (AFP); Kobal
Collection p. 26 (Rogue Pictures/Chen Jinquan);
Nature Picture Library p. 29 bottom (Eric Baccega);
Reuters pp. 8 (Beawiharta Beawiharta), 12 (Romeo
Ranoco); Science Photo Library p. 17 bottom (Tony
Craddock); Topfoto p. 14. Illustration on p. 17 top
by Tim Mayer.

The front cover shows a skull and crossbones, the
symbol used to warn of death and danger (Alamy/
Pick and Mix Images).

Every effort has been made to contact copyright
holders of material reproduced in this book. Any
omissions will be rectified in subsequent printings if
notice is given to the publishers.

CONTENTS

Abbreviations kg stands for kilograms • **lb** stands for pounds

Toxic!

Through the ages, people have mixed materials to try to make food taste better and stay fresh longer. Sometimes, their experiments went horribly wrong.

When materials are mixed, the ingredients can change in unexpected ways. It is hard to tell what will happen.

In the past, **toxic** substances were often added to food so it would keep for longer. Sadly, it didn't always make the people who ate it last longer. They often died!

Bakers in the 19th century: amazingly, toxic ingredients were often added to bread.

Bright toxic bread

In December 1859, an English baker added a sprinkling of what he thought was **chrome** yellow to brighten his bread. In fact, the colouring was a poison called **arsenic**. Six people died before his mistake was discovered.

arsenic   an extremely poisonous powder

4

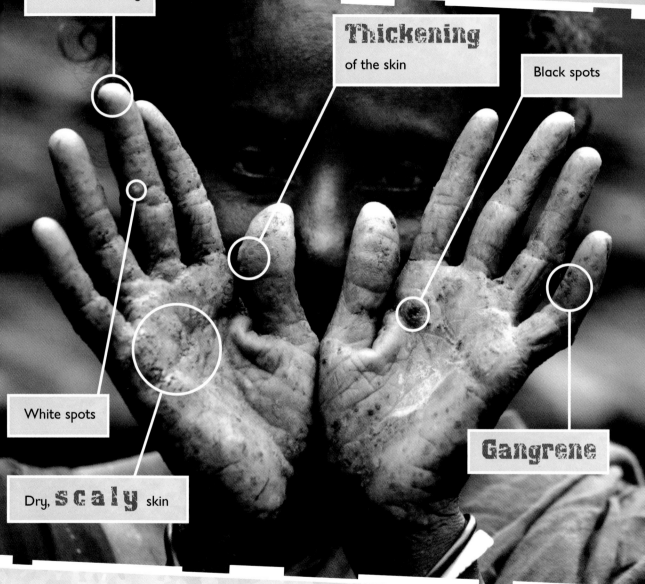

Tingling
fingertips or loss of feeling

Arsenic poisoning has terrible effects on the body and often leads to a painful death.

Thickening
of the skin

Black spots

White spots

Dry, **scaly** skin

Gangrene

chrome metallic substance used in dyes **toxic** poisonous

Kill or cure?

Beware! There could be poisons lurking in the park. Both dangerous poisons and useful medicines can be found in plants. You need to know which is which!

From ancient times, plants have been used to cure as well as kill. Arnica is a mountain plant. The petals are used to make gel to soothe bruises, stiffness and muscle soreness. The leaves are crushed to make ointment to ease **inflammation**. The whole plant is used to make pain-relieving tablets. But some plants – such as hemlock – cause pain instead of easing it.

Arnica growing on a mountainside.

inflammation   soreness or swelling

6

The seeds contain the strongest poison.

Stinky!

This is poison hemlock. The plant has a horrible smell of mice.

The leaves look like parsley,

People sometimes mistake the fleshy white roots for parsnips and eat them.

Death by hemlock

The famous Greek philosopher Socrates was put to death by poisoning. He was forced to swallow a drink made from the poison, hemlock.

Hemlock is often found in soggy soil, near streams and ditches.

Old wives' tales

How would you like to try this cure for flu? Catch a live fish, hold it in your mouth, and then throw it back in the river.

This Indonesian man's face is covered in hundreds of live honey bees – as part of a treatment to relieve pain!

People used to think the fish would take the sickness with it. It didn't. Some old wives' tales are nonsense. Other cures do work – although people in the past often didn't understand why.

Have you ever been stung by a bee? Bet it was painful. But strangely, bee stings to the face can help to treat pain and **diabetes**.

Veg under the bed

Placing half an onion under the bed of a sick person was said to draw away fever and poisons. It did nothing of the sort!

diabetes   when the body can't control sugar in the blood

Warts are small **bumps** that can form on the skin.

An **enzyme** in banana skin attacks warts.

Common warts are rough, grey-brown and dome-shaped.

Beware!
Warts can spread easily.

One old wives' tale says you can cure warts with a banana skin — which is actually true!

enzyme   a tiny substance that speeds up chemical reactions in living things

Dodgy anaesthetics

Imagine having an operation with no anaesthetic to put you to sleep. The surgeon starts sawing your leg with a sharp knife as you howl with pain.

To stop patients from screaming in agony during surgery, doctors used to mix substances from plants and metals to use as painkillers. But if your surgeon gave you the wrong mixture or too much of it, you might not wake up afterwards!

AMPUTATION

In this 18th-century operation, a surgeon cuts off a man's leg at the knee without anaesthetic.

Painkillers

Centuries ago, extracts from henbane and mandrake plants were used to stop pain. Henbane made people sleepy and forgetful. Mandrake slowed the heart rate and dulled pain. Both were deadly if you took too much.

anaesthetic drug that stops you feeling pain   **surgeon** doctor who carries out operations

As a painkiller, doctors sometimes used opium, which comes from the poppy flower. It numbs pain. Opium can make people ill though, or even kill them. People use opium as an illegal drug, with these terrible effects:

Death!

Heart may stop, and the person will die

Bad skin

Itchy and sweaty

Moody

Mood changes, unclear thoughts, no concentration, **hallucinations**

Sick

Sickness, no appetite

Sleepy

Eyelids heavy, sleepiness, blurred vision

Opium smokers in New York, USA, in 1926.

hallucinations seeing or hearing things that are not really there

11

Toxic shops

In the Middle Ages (from the 5th to the 15th century), apothecaries were people who sold medicines and the ingredients to make other medicines. You had to shop carefully. Some of them were deadly poisons.

These children in the Phillipines in 2005 are ill from cyanide poisoning.

Until 1617, apothecaries and grocers were the same people. Imagine buying celery in the same place as **cyanide**!

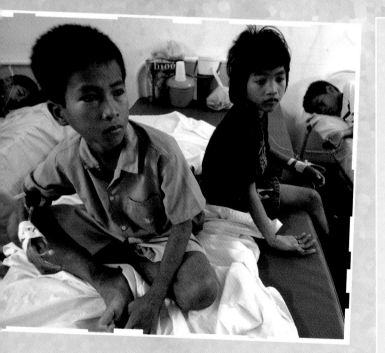

A dizzy mix

Back in the Middle Ages, if your gran had high blood pressure, she might have sent you to the apothecary to buy a jar of cyanide. This mixture of carbon and nitrogen would lower her blood pressure – but would make her weak and dizzy. If gran took too much, she'd stop breathing and die.

cyanide a highly poisonous chemical substance   **mercury** poisonous silver-white liquid metal

Foxglove was for people with heart problems. It strengthened the heart muscles but could also cause severe sickness and death.

Snake oil was applied to soothe sores, but caused vomiting and stomach aches.

Mercury was for wounds and rheumatism, but also caused deafness, blindness, liver disease, kidney failure and death.

People took absinthe if they had worms, but it also caused hallucinations and death.

A 15th-century apothecary's shop. The jars would have contained different medicines.

absinthe a strong, liquorice-flavoured alcoholic drink   **rheumatism** stiff and painful joints

Deaf and dying

When you go to the doctor, you expect to get better. Yet the world-famous composer, Ludwig van Beethoven, was killed by his own doctor. What happened?

A portrait of Beethoven writing his music.

The doctor saw Beethoven had a lung infection. Like other 19th-century doctors, he treated his patient with lead salts.

Beethoven didn't get better. Not only that, but he became completely deaf – the worse thing that can happen to a music lover. His doctor had no idea why. On 26 March 1827, the composer died, aged 56.

Dead locks

After Beethoven died, his friends visited his open coffin to pay their respects. As was the custom in those days, some took locks of their dead friend's hair to keep.

Headaches and severe pain

Zzzz Zzzz
Being tired but finding it hard to sleep

Pardon? Hearing problems

Duh!
Brain stops working properly

Not eating properly

Get off!
Behaviour problems – being aggressive and becoming annoyed easily

Lack of energy

Kidney damage

Two centuries later, scientists checked locks of hair from Beethoven's head. They were full of lead. The composer had died from lead poisoning, not from his illnesses. It had made him deaf and destroyed his body.

The effects of lead poisoning on Beethoven's body.

Big bang!

One of the most disastrous recipes ever was invented in 9th-century China. A cook accidentally mixed together the materials for gunpowder. That meal really did go off with a bang!

The cook squashed three ingredients into a bamboo tube: charcoal, sulphur and potassium. He put the tube on his fire to heat up. With a huge bang, a bright flash and the stink of bad eggs, it exploded!

The cook was trying to discover how to make the Chinese emperor live forever. Instead, he invented gunpowder. It was later used to fire guns.

The Chinese were the first to enjoy fireworks displays.

Fireworks of fear

The Chinese made the first fireworks by the 10th century. They stuffed bamboo tubes with gunpowder and lit them. They believed the loud explosion would frighten off evil spirits and ghosts.

ignites sets fire to

Instead of bamboo tubes, modern fireworks are made from a paper tube. Tiny balls of chemicals, called "**stars**", are dropped in and gunpowder is poured around them. When the fuse burns, it **ignites** the material around it, making the firework explode into showers of sparks.

Fuse

Paper tube

Black powder (gunpowder)

Small amount of explosive

Stars (burn to make bright colours)

The inside of a modern firework.

Modern fireworks exploding in bright colours.

stars   balls of chemicals that burn, making bright colours and sparks

17

Killer sweets!

It was 1958, in England. Shoppers queued at William Hardaker's market stall to buy their favourite sweet treat — mint humbugs. Little did they know that the sweets contained arsenic. Soon, 20 of them lay dead while 200 were seriously ill.

Merry drinkers in a 19th-century English pub.

Sweet but toxic

In the 19th century, many people liked their wine to taste sweet. **Lead acetate** was cheaper than sugar and had a sweet taste. Cheeky wine makers often mixed poisonous lead with the grapes as they **fermented**.

lead acetate   a poisonous white solid   **fermented**   changed from sugar to alcohol

Deadly

Each sweet contained enough arsenic to kill two people.

Killers

Hardaker sold enough sweets to kill 2,000 people.

Toxic

Hardaker sold 2 kg (5 lbs) of toxic sweets from his stall.

Humbugs were made of peppermint oil, sugar and gum. Because sugar was expensive, many sweet makers also added other cheaper substances to sweets, such as **plaster of Paris**. The man who sold the humbugs to Hardaker had accidentally added arsenic.

"Humbug Billy" (as William Hardaker was known) sold humbugs that looked like this but hid a nasty surprise.

plaster of Paris   a white powder that forms a paste when mixed with water and hardens quickly

In the past, paints were often made from mixtures of poisonous chemicals. Licking or eating them could kill. Even in the air, they were dangerous. Many artists became ill or died — poisoned by their paints.

Emerald green (fainting, sickness)

Chrome green (stomach pains, vomiting)

Chrome yellow (stomach pains, vomiting)

Bone black

Ultramarine

Red ochre

Cerulean blue

Chrome orange (cough, shortness of breath, sickness)

Lead white (sickness, headaches, weak muscles)

The paint palette of 19th-century painter Édouard Manet. He had no idea that it contained poisons.

Dead beautiful

It's true that looks can kill! In the past, women used toxic lead, mercury and acids in make-up.

In Tudor times, women painted their face with white lead to make it look pale and smooth. Rather than looking beautiful, they soon became ugly and ill. Their hair fell out, their skin rotted and they got stomach problems.

Modern make-up may be good for hiding spots. But is it always good in other ways?

A painting of a 19th-century woman putting on make-up.

Murderous make-up

Arsenic also gave the skin a pale look. In 17th-century Italy, Mrs Toffana sold make-up made from this poison to ladies. More than 600 men died after kissing their wives' arsenic-covered cheeks. Mrs Toffana was arrested as an evil poisoner and put to death.

Licking lips

Today, the average woman consumes about 2 kg (6 lbs) of lipstick during her life.

Burns!

Coal tar in some hair dyes can burn the skin.

Damage

Some lipsticks contain a chemical that can cause liver and kidney damage.

Rashes

Some blushers can trigger skin complaints.

Lung disorder

Some nail varnish can cause breathing problems.

Queens of poison

The plants belladonna and foxglove were popular poisons in the Middle Ages. In Shakespeare's tragic love story, *Romeo and Juliet*, Juliet fakes her death with a small dose of belladonna.

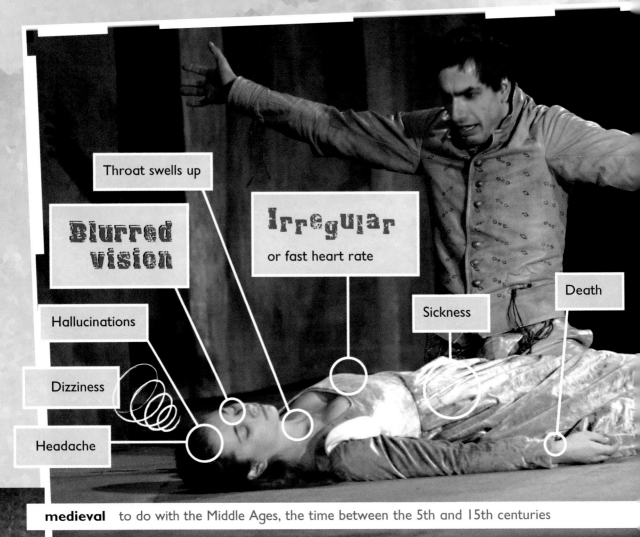

Throat swells up

Blurred vision

Irregular or fast heart rate

Hallucinations

Death

Sickness

Dizziness

Headache

medieval   to do with the Middle Ages, the time between the 5th and 15th centuries

Juliet has taken belladonna, also known as deadly nightshade. A large dose of this is definitely deadly!

The Italian Catherine de' Medici married a French king in the 16th century. She was an expert at mixing poisons with food.

A handy poison

It is said that Catherine de' Medici gave her enemy Jeanne a pair of gloves soaked with poison. Soon after, Jeanne was taken ill and died.

Romeo thinks his beautiful girlfriend has died. He drinks a foxglove potion and drops dead.

Medieval plotters found that poisoning was the perfect way to kill their enemies. It was so much less obvious than stabbing them to death.

Lucrezia Borgia and her brother Cesare lived in Italy in the late 15th and early 16th centuries. It is said that they poisoned people with a white powder made from arsenic and **phosphorus**. Lucrezia wore a ring filled with the poison mixture, ready to tip it into enemies' food.

phosphorus   a poisonous chemical that burns in air

Sabotage!

Surely those nasty poisoners were all in the distant past? Sadly, that's not quite true ...

Death of a master

Huo Yuan Jia was a Kung Fu Master. He won every competition until his sudden death in 1910. Years later, his body was dug up. The police found black spots on his **pelvis**, which showed he had been poisoned with arsenic. Had one of his opponents killed him? No one will ever know.

In 2004, Ukrainian politician Viktor Yushchenko was campaigning to be president. One day, he was rushed to hospital suffering from stomach pains. His organs were swollen, and lumps and blisters appeared on his face. Scientists discovered that Yushchenko had been poisoned by toxic chemicals called **dioxins**. Yushchenko survived and became president the following year.

In this shot from a film about Huo Yuan Jia, the actor shows the great master in action (right).

dioxins   chemicals used in industry and farming; most are poisonous

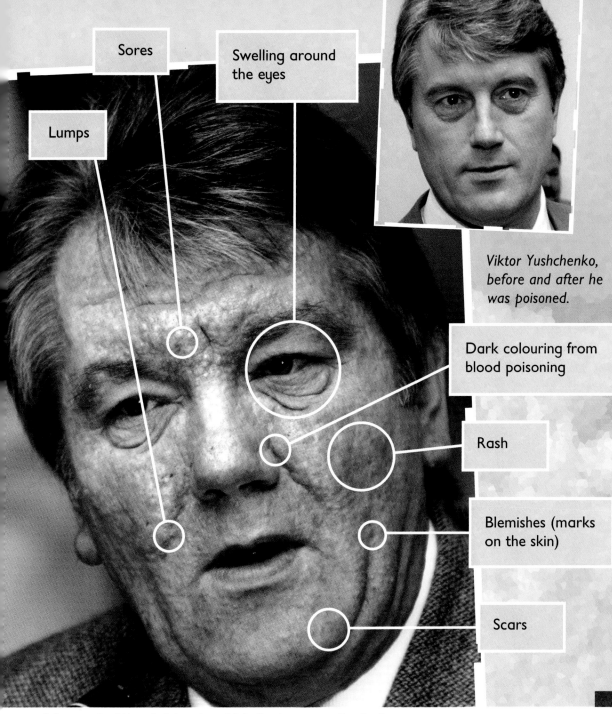

Sores

Swelling around the eyes

Lumps

Viktor Yushchenko, before and after he was poisoned.

Dark colouring from blood poisoning

Rash

Blemishes (marks on the skin)

Scars

pelvis part of the skeleton to which the legs are attached

Delivering the deadly dose

The average poisoner tricks the victim into eating or drinking a toxic mix. This is not the only method. Victims might breathe in poison – or even be shot with it.

A Kalahari Bushman from Namibia, southern Africa, makes a poisoned arrow for hunting.

Poisoned arrows can be used for hunting and fighting. They are made from toxic parts of plants and animals. In South America, poison from the skin of the arrow poison frog turns arrows into fatal weapons.

1 The man squeezes the poison from a **chrysalis**.

2 He carefully applies the poison just below the arrow tip.

3 The sharp arrow head will pierce the animal's body.

Poison gas

When toxic gas is released, it spreads far and wide in the air. In 1984 in Bhopal, India, poisonous gas was accidentally released from a factory. More than 2,000 people died from breathing it in, and many others were injured.

A woman injured by gas in Bhopal wearing eye patches.

Hunters in Indonesia firing bows and arrows.

chrysalis an insect while it is in a hard case changing into an adult

Glossary

absinthe a strong, liquorice-flavoured alcoholic drink

anaesthetic drug that stops you feeling pain

arsenic an extremely poisonous powder

chrome metallic substance used in dyes

chrysalis an insect while it is in a hard case changing into an adult

cyanide a highly poisonous chemical substance

diabetes when the body can't control sugar in the blood

dioxins chemicals used in industry and farming; most are poisonous

enzyme a tiny substance that speeds up chemical reactions in living things

fermented changed from sugar to alcohol

hallucinations seeing or hearing things that are not really there

ignites sets fire to

inflammation soreness or swelling

lead acetate a poisonous white solid

medieval to do with the Middle Ages, the time between the 5th and 15th centuries

mercury poisonous silver-white liquid metal

pelvis part of the skeleton to which the legs are attached

phosphorus a poisonous chemical that burns in air

plaster of Paris a white powder that forms a paste when mixed with water and hardens quickly

radioactive sending out powerful and dangerous rays

rheumatism stiff and painful joints

stars balls of chemicals that burn, making bright colours and sparks

surgeon doctor who carries out operations

toxic poisonous

Further information

Books

The Elements of Murder, A History of Poison by John Emsley (Oxford University Press, 2005) Includes interesting snippets of history and science about poisons and poisoners.

Horrible Science: Measly Medicine by Nick Arnold (Scholastic Hippo, 2006) A light-hearted look at the history of healthcare.

Horrible Science: Painful Poison by Nick Arnold (Scholastic Hippo, 2004) Funny tales about poisons.

Poisons by Peter Macinnis (Arcade Publishing, 2005) A history of poisons and poisoners.

Scientific Blunders by Robert Youngson (Constable & Robinson Limited, 1998) Reveals some of the mistakes that have been made by scientists.

Swindled: From Poison Sweets to Counterfeit Coffee – The Dark History of the Food Cheats by Bee Wilson (John Murray, 2008) How swindlers have tampered with our food throughout history.

Websites

www.bbc.co.uk/schools/ gcsebitesize/history/ shp/modern/ indrevsurgeryrev1.shtml A BBC Bitesize site about 19th-century surgery.

www.bbc.co.uk/ health/conditions/ poisonousplants1.shtml A site on poisonous plants and how to recognize them, on BBC Health.

www.yesnet.yk.ca/ schools/projects/ renaissance/borgia.html An introduction to the Borgia family, who lived in Italy in the 15th and 16th centuries.

www.ukhairdressers. com/history%20of%20 beauty.asp Toxic cosmetics through the ages.

Index